SHIRE NATUR⧸

CW00971763

THE BARN OWL
IAIN R. TAYLOR

CONTENTS

Cover: *Barn owl showing characteristic facial disc.*

Series editor: Jim Flegg.

Printed in Great Britain by CIT Printing Services,
Press Buildings, Merlins Bridge, Haverfordwest, Dyfed SA61 1XF.

Introduction

The barn owl (*Tyto alba alba*) is a strikingly beautiful species and although once a familiar sight in the British countryside is now rather uncommon. It feeds mostly on small mammals which it detects by sound and catches in its long, sharp claws. For its body size it has relatively long wings which give increased lift and enable it to fly slowly when hunting. The legs are also extremely long allowing it to penetrate deep into vegetation when catching its prey.

There are many regional names for the barn owl but white owl and screech owl are widely used. The latter is taken from its most frequently heard call: a long drawn out scream most often delivered in flight. However, it has a very wide vocal repertoire including numerous variations on the scream, hisses and 'snoring'. The snore is a throaty wheezing noise, often very persistent, given mostly during the breeding season by the young and the female and less frequently by the male. It is often given by the female and young when begging for food and by the female during courtship activities, and can be surprisingly loud.

Male and female barn owls do not differ in size, measuring about 33 to 35 cm from head to tail. Males generally weigh around 330 grams whereas the weight of the females varies seasonally, being about 400 grams during the breeding season, falling to about 360 grams during the winter months. In plumage males are generally lighter coloured than females. Their upper parts especially are paler and less heavily marked. They usually have less distinct wing and tail bars and in extreme cases can lack these altogether. About 98 per cent of males are completely white underneath whereas females nearly always have small black flecks, in some cases restricted to the flanks but often over the entire underparts. Juveniles are similar to adults except that many start life with distinctly buff underparts. In the case of males this is normally just a faint wash across the chest but it can be very rich in the females and sometimes extend over the whole underbody. Some young females are so deeply coloured they appear indistinguishable from the dark continental race *Tyto alba guttata* and one wonders how many of the reports of this sub-species in Britain actually refer to juvenile females of the British race. The plumage of both males and females tends to become paler with age and some very old females can be inseparable from males.

Most people will have seen photographs of the barn owl but in the wild it can be very elusive. For most of the year it is nocturnal and selects undisturbed hidden places for roosting during the day. Occasionally a quick glimpse may be had in car headlights. For those who want better views the best times to watch for them are in winter, when they are sometimes forced to hunt during the day, and in midsummer, when they may be seen carrying prey to their young in late evening. Clues to their presence may often be obtained by finding moulted feathers or their characteristic black shiny pellets in farm buildings. However, care should always be taken not to disturb the birds especially when they are nesting; indeed barn owls are afforded special protection by the Wildlife and Countryside Act and a licence from the Nature Conservancy Council is needed to visit nests. It is better to locate potential nest sites during the winter and then observe the birds from a safe distance during the breeding season.

Range, habitat and density

The barn owl is one of the most widespread of all bird species. It is found throughout Europe, from Scotland and Denmark southwards, in the Middle East and most of Africa, India, south-east Asia and Australia and North, Central and South America. Some 35 sub-species have been described. It is absent from northern and high-altitude areas where winter weather conditions are too severe and it also tends to avoid dense tropical forests and extreme desert habitats. In

1. *Geographical distribution of the barn owl.*

2. *The amount of dark flecking on the underparts is the most reliable characteristic for distinguishing the sexes. About 98 per cent of males have no markings (top left) whereas 97 per cent of females have extensive markings (bottom row). A small proportion of males and females have just a few flecks (top right) and are difficult to separate.*

3

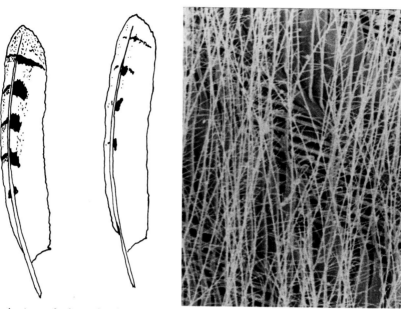

3. *Typical primary feathers of male and female barn owls. Those of the female (left) are dark and strongly marked whereas the male's (right) are much paler and lightly marked.*

4. *The surface of a barn owl feather. The photograph was taken with a scanning electron microscope and shows the long, hair-like extensions of the barbules which give the feathers their soft velvety feel.*

Britain it is sedentary, but in many areas large-scale movements are undertaken in response to changes in prey abundance. In North America the most northerly populations perform regular southward migrations for distances up to 2000 km (1240 miles) to avoid harsh winters.

Throughout its range the barn owl prefers open or lightly wooded country. In the natural state this would include grasslands, wetlands, savannahs and semi-arid areas. However, it has benefited greatly from the activities of man and utilises all but the most intensive farmland as well as plantation crops such as oil-palm, dates and coconut. In Britain young conifer plantations can be ideal habitats.

For nesting, a hole of some kind is generally needed. In populated areas this is often found in buildings such as lofts and haysheds but elsewhere holes in trees or cliffs are normally used. In Britain there is a marked geographical difference in the relative use made of nest sites in trees and in buildings. In drier eastern areas tree holes are most frequently used whereas in western areas buildings are used more. It has been suggested that barn owls actively select buildings in the west because they offer greater protection from the rain. However, in detailed studies in Scotland it was found that the owls simply used the two types of nest site according to their availability. In the western areas large oaks and elms, the main tree species used, were much less abundant than in the east. Conversely, derelict and disused farm buildings were more abundant in the west reflecting the less profitable farming conditions there. Similar conclusions were reached in a study of barn owls in Wales.

In the savannahs of Africa barn owls frequently use the huge stick nests of the Hammerkop (*Scopus umbretta*). These domed structures can be as much as 1.5 metres across and can last many years.

In some areas, when prey is abundant but nest sites are in short supply, barn

5. *A typical female barn owl showing the richly coloured upper parts and flecked underparts.*

6. *A typical male barn owl showing pale upper parts and completely white underparts.*

owls may nest gregariously. As many as fifty pairs have been found together. The term colony cannot strictly be used to describe these aggregations as there is no evidence that the pairs cooperate with each other in any way. Normally pairs nest apart but, unlike species such as the sparrowhawk (*Accipiter nisus*), there seems to be no strict spacing, distances probably being determined mainly by the availability of suitable nest sites.

There is little information on the density of breeding barn owls in Britain or elsewhere. Finding all the pairs in a particular area is very difficult and time-consuming and has seldom been attempted. In southern Scotland, where the author has studied barn owls in detail over many years, numbers vary greatly in response to fluctuations in prey abundance. A sample of 22 areas each measuring 10 by 10 km gave an average density of 5.1 pairs per 100 square km in the years when the birds were most abundant and 2.5 pairs per 100 square km when the population was at its lowest. The maximum density found was 12 pairs per 100 square km.

The range of six pairs nesting in farm-land in southern Scotland was determined using radio-tracking. This averaged about 3.23 square km per pair. The ranges of some adjacent pairs overlapped extensively and some birds were seen hunting within about 100 metres of their neighbours' nest with no obvious aggression between the birds. The nest site itself seems to be vigorously defended, however, and prolonged battles have been observed between occupiers and intruders.

Feeding habits

Throughout its range in western Europe the barn owl is a small mammal hunter. To help it catch these prey it has astonishingly acute hearing. The heart-shaped face so characteristic of the species is basically an elaborate hearing aid. It is formed by two oval concave discs of short stiff feathers. These are attached to

7. *A male carrying a short-tailed vole to the nest.*

the top of the head, which is normally held at right angles to its neck. The discs serve to funnel sound waves into the ear drum in much the same way as the ear pinnae of mammals. An asymmetrical arrangement of the ear openings enables direction to be determined. The whole system is so effective that barn owls are able to locate and capture prey in total darkness. Good hearing is probably needed under all light conditions, however, as the prey are usually hidden in rank vegetation. It can also be extremely useful in winter when prey may be hidden underneath a layer of snow. Several species of owl can detect and catch prey through snow and this is especially important for species such as the great grey owl (*Strix nebulosa*) which have to contend with long hard winters.

The eye of the barn owl is specially modified to operate well under conditions of poor light. The retina has a high density of rods which are particularly sensitive to low light intensities. The eye is elongated with an exceptionally large cornea and lens which ensures that the maximum amount of light enters the eye and falls on the retina. The frontal position of the eyes provides good binocular vision which, in addition to

giving improved distance perception, also enhances sensitivity by gathering more visual information. Thus, when it is too dark for the human eye to operate, the eyes of owls can still provide detailed information about their environment. The fact that barn owls often hunt during the day demonstrates that their eyes also function in daylight but probably they have poorer colour vision and resolution in daylight than diurnal birds.

The most commonly seen hunting technique involves a slow deliberate quartering of open rough areas, usually at a height of about 2 to 4 metres, pausing frequently to hover or hang in the wind. Long wide wings give the owl a very low wing loading. Hair-like extensions of the barbules give the feather surfaces a soft velvety feel and it has been suggested that this reduces flight noise enabling the owl to detect the slightest sound from its prey and to make a noiseless approach. The distinctive white underparts are probably important in flight hunting during daylight, helping to obscure the bird's outline against the sky in much the same way as does the white plumage of seabirds.

Barn owls also frequently hunt from perches and on farmland they can be seen working their way systematically along

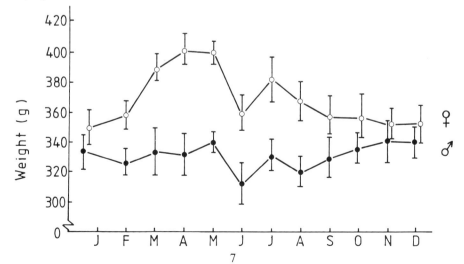

Egg laying											
Incubation											
Feeding young in nest											
Feeding young out of nest											
Adult males moulting											
Adult females moulting											

| Jan | Feb | Mar | Apr | May | Jun | Jul | Aug | Sept | Oct | Nov | Dec |

8. *The annual cycle of the barn owl in Britain, showing the timing of breeding and moult.*

fence lines, pausing for several minutes on a post to scan the surrounding area. Perch hunting seems to be especially important in winter probably because the owls need to conserve as much energy as possible at this time. Pouncing can occur directly from the perch but usually the bird takes to the air, often hovering momentarily before descending on the prey. The descent is normally rather slow and controlled with the wings held back above the body and the neck noticeably extended. Frequent adjustments are made and the bird may suddenly change course or seemingly somersault. At the last minute the legs are brought well

9. *Annual weight changes of adult male and female barn owls. The sexes do not differ significantly during the winter months but in early spring the females start to accumulate reserves and reach a maximum weight during laying. Both sexes lose weight significantly when feeding young but recover rapidly.*

10. *This head-on shot of a barn owl shows clearly the long wings.*

11. *Barn owl leg and foot showing the long needle-sharp talons and papillae which help to give a stronger grip.*

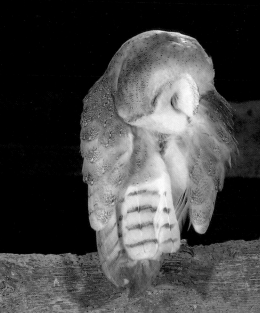

12. *Adult male at tree hole nest site.*

13. *Adult female preening.*

forward in front of the head and the claws are spread. Sometimes, presumably when the first attempt failed, the birds may run along the ground in pursuit. Small mammals are normally swallowed whole on the spot but may be carried back to the nest in the talons to feed the young.

Little is known about the factors that affect hunting success. Heavy rain seems to inhibit activity, presumably because the soft plumage is easily wetted. It might also be expected that strong winds would reduce hunting success but this has not been studied. Deep snow or even thinner iced snow clearly presents difficulties. Access to the prey is cut off and some winter mortality occurs through starvation at such times. Small mammals such as voles seem little affected by snow and are able to survive well even under a thick covering. Intense cold without snow is considerably worse for them as they then have little insulation against heat loss.

For most of the year barn owls are nocturnal but when feeding young, especially when food is scarce, they can be seen hunting for two or three hours before dark and again around dawn. If there has been a succession of very wet nights or if prey abundance is low, they may even hunt throughout the whole day. Daytime hunting is quite frequent in winter during spells of severe weather and when conditions are clear but intensely cold. This may be a behavioural adaptation to conserve energy as the heat loss through radiation to the cold night sky would be very great were the birds to hunt at night under such conditions.

The significance of the barn owl's plumage coloration has often been puzzled over. The importance of the white underparts has already been discussed. The upper parts are mainly buff but with many delicate black and grey markings. These tend to be arranged in lines up and down the back, giving a striated appearance. It seems likely that this functions as camouflage against predators during daytime hunting. When perched, the eyes and ears are orientated forwards leaving the bird vulnerable to attack from behind. The bird's markings blend in remarkably well against a background of grass stems.

Barn owls nearly always swallow their prey whole, unlike diurnal birds of prey which usually tear their food up before swallowing. The digestive juices of owls

9

are also considerably less acidic than those of most diurnal raptors. This means that barn owls take in large amounts of bone and fur which they are unable to digest. This material is retained in the forepart of the gut during digestion then compressed into a tight mass by muscular action and regurgitated as pellets.

Pellets from barn owls vary greatly in size from about 2 cm long to as much as 10 cm. The best places to look for them are buildings such as haysheds and old barns that are regularly used as roosting sites. Accumulations of pellets build up on the ground underneath favourite perches and on top of bales of hay or straw. Care must be taken not to disturb nesting birds so it is best to investigate during the winter months. Fresh moist pellets can easily be teased apart but older, dried up specimens should first be soaked for several days. By careful dissection the indigestible parts of the owls' prey can be recovered. With skill, completely intact

skulls of small mammals can be removed. Pellets are thus a convenient and reliable source of information on diet and, interestingly, can also yield valuable evidence on the distribution of some of our rarer small mammals.

The food of barn owls varies regionally and according to habitat. In most places in Britain the short-tailed vole (*Microtus agrestis*) predominates, although in some areas brown rats (*Rattus norvegicus*), common shrews (*Sorex araneus*) or wood mice (*Apodemus sylvaticus*) may be more important. The short-tailed vole is a grassland species and in lowland areas it occurs in permanent grass fields and hay meadows as well as along the banks of rivers and ditches, woodland edges, hedges and road verges. In the uplands it is very widespread on sheep-walks and rough grazings and extremely high abundances are found in young coniferous plantations. It is active throughout the day as well as at night but shows

10

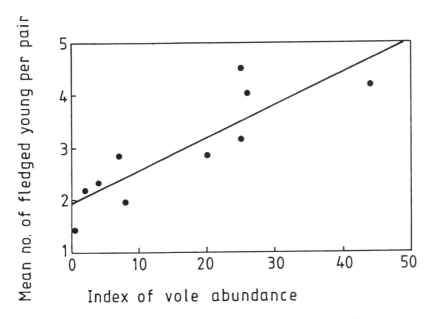

15. *The average number of young reared by barn owls is very closely related to the abundance of its main prey species, the short-tailed vole. Data from southern Scotland.*

16. *The overwinter mortality of adult barn owls is closely related to the abundance of short-tailed voles. Data from southern Scotland.*

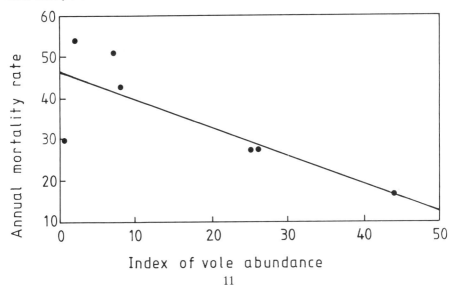

17. *Female barn owl on the nest.*

18. *A clutch of nine barn owl eggs.*

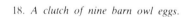

19. *Male with a brood of three young in an old hay loft.*

20. *Newly fledged barn owl showing the buff chest.*

peaks of activity at dusk and dawn. Its numbers fluctuate cyclically, usually over a three to five year period, and these year to year changes are reflected in its contribution to the barn owls' diet as well as many other aspects of the owls' biology discussed later. At times of peak abundance this single species can constitute up to 95 per cent of the diet of barn owls nesting in coniferous plantations. During the spring the owls capture a disproportionately large number of male short-tailed voles. At this time the voles are very active in defence of their territories and males range over a much greater area than females. This presumably exposes them to a much greater predation risk.

A relative of the short-tailed vole, the bank vole (*Clethrionomys glareolus*) is taken much less frequently, presumably because its preference for thick scrubby cover makes it less available to barn owls. In Ireland the bank vole was first discovered in 1964 (presumably having been introduced) and where it occurs it is now an important item in the diet of local barn owls. Short-tailed voles are absent from Ireland and it is possible that bank voles have been able to expand their habitat into more open areas as a result but have, in the process, become more vulnerable to predation. The wood mouse is usually an important prey in lowland habitats. As its alternative name, the long-tailed field mouse, suggests this species is not at all restricted to woodland and is found in similar habitats to the short-tailed vole, except that it is much less common in upland areas. In Ireland the wood mouse often becomes the most important prey item. On the mainland of Britain barn owls seem to take the wood mouse less frequently than its abundance might suggest. A likely explanation is that the wood mouse is a very active jumper and runner and reacts very quickly to danger so it may be rather difficult to catch. Common shrews are taken most where grassland such as old pastures, meadows and rough grazing predominate.

In addition to small mammals a range of other species is taken, especially when mammals are scarce. In early spring common frogs (*Rana temporaria*) are sometimes caught and in summer small birds such as house sparrow (*Passer*

domesticus), starling (*Sturnus vulgaris*), swallow (*Hirundo rustica*) and meadow pipit (*Anthus pratensis*) may be taken. Mostly these are young inexperienced birds. Invertebrates, especially beetles, may feature sometimes but always in small amounts. Interestingly earthworms, that are so prominent in the diet of the tawny owl (*Strix aluco*) and kestrel (*Falco tinnunculus*), seem to be completely avoided.

Barn owls pose no threat whatsoever to game birds and only the most ignorant of gamekeepers now think otherwise. However, they may sometimes become serious predators of other species. In 1949 the Cape barn owl (*Tyto alba affinis*) was introduced into the Seychelle Islands in the hope that it would help control rats in coconut plantations. The birds flourished but unfortunately found some of the rare endemic mammals and seabirds such as the fairy tern (*Gygis alba*) more to their liking. Subsequent efforts to remove the owls have only been partly successful.

The daily food requirement of wild barn owls has not been properly determined but a number of estimates have been made for captive birds. These range from about 100 to 150 grams. Judging by their body weight a figure nearer 100 grams would seem the more likely. This could be provided by four to six average-sized voles.

Breeding and moulting

The breeding season for barn owls starts very early in the year. Some established pairs will have used their nest site for roosting during the winter, but even those that have roosted elsewhere pay regular nightly visits to their nest site. From February onwards activity around the nest begins to increase. The male in particular becomes more vocal, giving his long screeching call. For those whose mates have survived the winter the main function of this is probably to proclaim ownership of the site. For others it will also serve to attract potential mates. The male has a form of display flight usually involving much calling. It is concentrated close to the nest site although also given away from the nest. Male and female indulge in erratic, energetic chases often around as well as in and out of the potential nest. As time progresses courtship feeding becomes more important. Males who have not yet attracted mates usually store up food at their chosen sites and this may serve to impress on visiting females the quality of the male or of the habitat. It may also enable a male to respond quickly to the appearance of a female by presenting her with food. However food presentation is not of value simply during courtship. Before laying the females accumulate reserves, increasing their body weight by up to 25 per cent. Some of this is used up during egg formation but mostly it is used during incubation. The female does all the incubation and is fed by the male. Her reserves are an insurance against poor hunting conditions. In tawny owls it has been shown that the more reserves a female has at the start of incubation the less likely it is that she will have to leave the eggs to hunt for herself and hence the greater will be her breeding success.

For two or three weeks before laying and during laying most males roost with their mates at the nest site. The function of this is probably to defend the site and the mate and also to ensure that no other male fertilises the eggs. Once the clutch is complete most males move to a different roost which can be as much as 2 km from the nest.

Some barn owls in Britain still use the traditional nest sites in trees and cliffs but most now nest in close association with man, making use of farm buildings, dovecotes, chimneys, church towers, haysheds and almost any kind of disused and derelict building. The main requirements are freedom from frequent direct disturbance, easy access and a reasonably large floor space. They take readily to nest boxes sited in suitable locations. No actual nest is constructed but the accumulation of pellet debris may form a platform for the eggs.

The date of laying depends on year to year variations in vole abundance and the habitat around the nest site. Pairs nesting in young conifer plantations where vole densities are normally higher than elsewhere usually produce their first eggs in March or early April in years when the voles are at the peak of their cycle, but when voles are scarce the same pairs may not lay until May. In most years barn owls in arable farmland lay later than those in plantations. New pairs breeding for the first time sometimes lay as late as August. When food is abundant some pairs, usually those that have laid early, produce a second clutch in July or August. There are also two records from southern Scotland of females rearing a first brood with one male then laying a second clutch with another male at a completely different nest site.

The number of eggs laid also varies according to habitat and vole abundance. In plantations the clutch may be up to eight or nine eggs when voles are abundant but as low as three or four when voles are scarce. Birds in arable habitats usually have much smaller clutches, normally between two and five.

Incubation starts with the first egg. Laying is normally done on alternate days but may occasionally be interrupted by exceptionally severe weather and an extreme interval of sixteen days between eggs has been recorded. The eggs hatch asynchronously and it has been suggested that this results in a dominance hierarchy among the young, allowing at least the larger chicks to survive during times of food shortage. However, most mortality of young occurs when they are less than about fourteen days old, well before the peak food requirements of the brood. It is possible that asynchronous hatching serves to spread out the food requirements of the brood such that the peak demand is less than it would be if the chicks were all of the same age.

For the first two or three weeks after hatching the female stays at the nest with the chicks, brooding them and tearing up and giving them prey brought in by the male. When hunting has been good, surplus food may be cached at the nest and used as an insurance against poor conditions. Often, however, these items go uneaten and become trampled into the general nest debris. Eventually, when the chicks are older, the hen hunts as well.

21. *Barn owl chicks inside a hollow tree.*

22. *Pellets, droppings and moulted feathers underneath a frequently used barn owl roost.*

Often at this stage she moves to a roost away from the nest. The chicks can now swallow prey whole and visits by the parents may last only the few seconds needed to pass over prey. The young reach their maximum weight and complete their skeleton growth by about 35 days but the wing feathers are not fully grown until 60 to 65 days. After leaving the nest the young remain in the vicinity and are fed for a further two to four weeks, after which they disperse.

Barn owls can be remarkably successful in their breeding. When food is scarce some pairs do not lay, but once eggs are laid total failure is very rare. Of 356 nesting attempts recorded in southern Scotland by the author only 26 (7.3 per cent) were completely unsuccessful. Nine of these involved desertion before the clutch was completed, all but one in years of poor food supply. In seven cases all the eggs were infertile and failed to hatch, and in a further seven all the young died of starvation. The remaining three cases involved destruction of the nest site by humans.

The main sources of loss in successful nests are failure of eggs to hatch and

death of chicks. There is little evidence that predation from other species is important. Normally the chicks that die are the youngest members of the brood that have failed to grow as rapidly as the others. The percentage that die is related to vole abundance and is greater in habitats with poorer food supplies. This suggests that food shortage is the most important cause of death. However, young have also been found dying in nests where there was a fresh cache of surplus food and where the other chicks had full crops. Often the intact remains of dead young are found at the nest but sometimes they simply disappear or are found partly eaten. Some researchers have suggested that cannibalism is important and traces of chicks are, indeed, sometimes found in the pellets of other young. However, it is not known to what extent this represents true cannibalism or simply the eating of chicks after death.

The maximum recorded number of young in a single brood reared to fledging by a pair of barn owls in southern Scotland was nine, and another pair reared eleven in one season but in two broods. However, the average produc-

16

23. *An adult flies along the rafters of an old barn.*

tion of the whole population, excluding pairs that did not lay, was 4.1 per pair when voles were abundant but only 1.5 per pair when voles were scarce.

Most barn owls start breeding in their first year of life but some not until their second. Once settled at a site they are remarkably faithful to it. In southern Scotland 97 per cent of males and 94 per cent of females bred at the same site in successive years. This means that they remain at a site regardless of its quality even when an adjacent site in better quality habitat becomes available. In this respect the barn owl differs markedly from species, such as the sparrowhawk, in which individuals tend to move to better quality habitats as they become older.

In many countries barn owls appear to disperse widely after leaving the nest and may breed hundreds of kilometres away from their natal area. In Britain, however, they seem to be much more local. Usually information of this kind is obtained from birds ringed at the nest and subsequently found dead and re-ported by members of the public. With barn owls this presents some difficulty as

many are found dead on the roads. There are reports of birds being trapped on vehicles and ending up a long way from where they were hit. Thus it is difficult to say whether they moved a particular distance on their own or were trans-ported. However, in the study in south-ern Scotland ringed birds were caught and released alive at their nesting places and these records gave an average figure of 7.4 km (4.6 miles) for males and 9.1 km (5.6 miles) for females between their natal area and their subsequent breeding place.

MOULT

Moult in barn owls is a rather complex affair. At their first moult, when they are about a year old, most replace only a single primary feather, usually a central one. Thereafter moult proceeds in oppo-site directions towards the outer and inner edges of the wing away from the central primary. Usually only three or four primaries are shed each year so that most birds are three or four years old before their full juvenile set is replaced. The pattern of secondary and tail moult is even more complicated but again it usually takes two to three years to produce a completely new set.

Barn owl flight feathers are not particularly strong or hard wearing and are often very tattered and broken before they are replaced. One would imagine there must be some particularly compelling reason for not renewing them every year. Perhaps gradual replacement is an adaptation to a fluctuating and unpredictable food supply whilst attempting to retain as much wing efficiency as possible. Moult in birds is an extremely demanding process both in protein and energy and requires an increased consumption of prey. It may be important for barn owls, especially young and inexperienced ones, to spread this load as much as possible.

The moult occurs during the summer and autumn when prey populations are high and hunting conditions are at their best. However, breeding must also take place at this time and a compromise between the demands of moult and breeding has to be reached. Most females start replacing tail and secondary feathers, and often primaries, whilst they are incubating. At this time they are fed by their mates who do not yet have to attend to the demands of growing young. Thus a considerable proportion of the female's moult is completed before she joins in hunting to feed the chicks. Most males start replacing their tail feathers when the hen is incubating but delay moulting secondaries and primaries until the young are quite well grown. In both sexes moult is usually completed by the end of October.

Moult patterns and discarded feathers can be very useful when studying barn owl populations. The pattern of primary replacement can be used to tell the age of individuals, enabling the population to be divided into first year, second year and older birds. The relationship between age and other characteristics such as breeding performance can then be examined. The precise marking patterns on wing and tail feathers are unique to the individual bird and old feathers found around the nest or roost site can be used to tell if the same birds are present in successive years. They can also usually be used to identify the sex of a bird.

Mortality

There are reports of barn owls being taken by some predators such as peregrine falcon (*Falco peregrinus*) and goshawk (*Accipiter gentilis*), but generally they have rather few natural enemies. At one time they were persecuted by gamekeepers and much sought after by taxidermists but today these are probably of minor importance. The main causes of death seem to be starvation and accident. Many are killed on roads and railways and the numbers dying on roads has tended to increase with the number and speed of vehicles. However, the importance of this source of mortality is difficult to assess as many of the birds involved are well below average weight and may have been forced to feed along roadsides because of food shortage. How many of these would ultimately have died of starvation anyway is not known.

The heaviest mortality falls on young birds and there is a peak of deaths in their first autumn when they are learning to fend for themselves. Many probably die of starvation because they have not learnt to hunt effectively. A surprisingly large number are found drowned in water troughs. Estimates from East Germany and Switzerland give first-year mortality at about 70 per cent. In southern Scotland only 21 per cent survived to become recruited to the breeding populations when voles were abundant, and when voles were scarce the figure was even lower at 5 per cent.

The adults survive well during the summer months and most deaths occur in winter from December to February. There are very large variations from year to year in adult mortality rates and this is most closely related to changes in the abundance of short-tailed voles. For example, in young forestry plantations, sheep-walk and marginal hill areas where the birds are highly dependent on short-tailed voles as prey, winter mortality is about 53 per cent when voles are scarce but much lower, at 28 per cent, when voles are abundant. Mortality is not uniformly spread over the winter but tends to be concentrated during periods

of severe weather, particularly after prolonged windy and wet conditions and
after snowfall. Deep or frosted snow cuts
off the food supply and after about seven
to ten days of such conditions many die of
starvation. Strangely, adults do not move
in response to these conditions. It may be
more important for them to try to retain
possession of roost and nest sites. Mortality rates are related to the altitude at
which the birds live, reflecting the sever-
ity of winter weather. In southern Scotland, those living below 100 metres above
sea level experience on average about 20
per cent annual mortality whereas for
those above 200 metres the figure is
about 55 per cent. There is no difference
in the mortality rates of males and
females.

Some authors have concluded that
yearly fluctuations in barn owl breeding
numbers are brought about solely by
differences in the number of young produced, but there is little to support this
idea. Yearly variations in numbers in
southern Scotland are most strongly related to variations in the mortality rates
of adults and immatures associated with
fluctuations in the vole population. In
addition, exceptionally severe winters,
such as those experienced in Britain in
1962-3 and 1978-9, result in abnormally
high mortality through starvation and are
followed by population declines. In
southern Scotland, for example, the
1978-9 winter, which was characterised
by prolonged snow cover and extremely
low temperatures, was followed by a
decrease in the number of breeding pairs
of about 40 per cent. Fortunately the vole
population remained very high throughout. Had the severe conditions coincided
with a crash in the vole population, the
decline in owl numbers would have been
very much greater.

The significance of pesticides as a cause
of death in barn owls is not clearly
understood. Predators of birds and fish
are generally more seriously affected by
organochlorine pesticides than those that
prey mainly on mammals. This is because
mammal eaters are normally at the end of
a somewhat shorter food chain and there
is, therefore, less chance for pesticide
loads to accumulate. There is some evidence that some barn owls died as a

direct result of Dieldrin poisoning in the
early 1960s but this highly toxic organochlorine has been gradually phased out
since then. It has also been suggested that
rodenticides may have been responsible
for barn owl deaths in some parts of
Britain. Most modern rodenticides are
anticoagulants, that is they cause death
by internal haemorrhaging. The earliest
and most widely known of these is Warfarin, which has been in use since the
early 1950s. Warfarin is not particularly
toxic and can be metabolised by mammals so that many days of exposure are
needed to cause death. Owls come into
contact with rodenticides by eating rats or
mice that have already taken up the
poison but because of the low toxicity it is
unlikely that many barn owls were killed
by Warfarin. However, there was
another, more important, consequence of
low toxicity: rodents quickly developed a
genetic resistance to Warfarin. This led to
the introduction of the so-called second-
generation rodenticides (for example
difenacoum and bromadiolone) in the
mid 1970s. These are much more potent
than Warfarin and have been shown in
laboratory trials to be capable of poisoning barn owls. In recent years a small
number of dead barn owls have been
found in circumstances which suggest
rodenticide poisoning. The exact significance of second-generation rodenticides
as a cause of death in barn owls is still
unclear, but intensive research currently
being undertaken by the Institute of
Terrestrial Ecology should lead to a
better understanding.

Conservation

In most of Europe barn owl numbers
have declined quite markedly during the
twentieth century. Decreases have been
reported in France, Belgium, Denmark,
West Germany, Holland, Sweden,
Spain, Britain and Ireland. The cause is
undoubtedly change in the farmland
environment. Since the Second World
War farming methods have been re-
volutionised. The emphasis has been on
maximising production and efficiency and
this has been brought about by increased

19

24. *Barn owl at sunset.*

mechanisation, breeding of new crop varieties, land drainage and the use of inorganic fertilisers and pesticides. The result has been a widespread reduction in the area of suitable barn owl habitat.

The need for bigger fields, to allow the efficient operation of large machines, has meant the removal of hedges, ditches, woodlands and other edge areas which were important hunting places. Grassland is now managed much more intensively. Most of the old permanent pastures which were rich in prey for barn owls have been replaced by short-rotation grasslands. These are sown with a restricted range of high quality grasses, usually varieties of rye-grass, and much more use is made of fertiliser, giving very high quality grazing. Stocking rates are higher and the fields are grazed more uniformly. The result is a habitat that supports rather few small mammals.

A similar fate has befallen the old hay meadows which were also rich hunting grounds for the owls, providing a good food supply when they were rearing their young. Some hay is still grown for sheep feed but as cattle feed it has been largely replaced by silage. The main difference between the two is that hayfields are left undisturbed until they are cut in late summer whereas silage fields are subject to repeated mechanical operations. In early spring they may be rolled to encourage increased tillering. Then two and sometimes three cuts of grass are taken during the summer. There is thus little opportunity for small mammal populations to build up in silage fields.

In addition to changes in pastures and hayfields, many former areas of rough grazing have been upgraded and converted to cereal production or improved grasslands. Thus there has been a very widespread reduction in the amount of grassland habitat of the type barn owls need for hunting.

The advent of the combine harvester has brought about many changes that affect barn owls. Before their introduction, the corn was cut and left in stooks in the fields to dry. It was then stored in stacks in the stackyard adjacent to the farm buildings. Threshing was done three or four times over the winter when corn was needed. The stackyards usually sup-

20

ported high populations of rats and mice and many old farmers report that barn owls would often hunt there during the winter. They were probably a very important source of food in spells of severe weather and might have made the difference between survival and starvation. With modern combines the corn is cut, threshed and stored in rodent-proof containers all in one go, so the food supply for these small mammal pests is effectively removed. Other significant developments in cereal farming are stubble burning and autumn ploughing and sowing. There are now very few overwintering stubble fields and this must have reduced the abundance of small mammals still further.

In addition to all these changes affecting habitat for hunting, there has been a widespread reduction in the availability of suitable nest sites. Many trees have been removed during field enlargement and this has now been made worse by the widespread loss of elm, one of the most important nesting trees, through Dutch elm disease. Perhaps just as important, however, has been the change in farm buildings. Barn owls need a site that is relatively free from repeated disturbance. In traditional farm buildings there were many lofts and odd corners that fulfilled this need. When horses were in use, large quantities of hay had to be stored for winter food and this was usually left to mature for a year or two. Thus nearly all farms had hay lofts that were undisturbed during the summer months and these made ideal nesting places. Large modern open-plan buildings are in constant use and subject to too much disturbance. Many of the old buildings have been pulled down or converted, in some cases into dwelling houses.

It is not surprising, then, with all these adverse changes, that barn owls have declined, but is there any hope for the future? Can barn owls survive with modern agriculture? The answer might be found by studying areas where the species is still holding its own. Such an area in southern Scotland was examined in detail by the author. It consisted of about 300 square km (120 square miles) of lowland farmland predominantly devoted to livestock rearing and dairy production but with some areas of cereal. The farming was modern and quite intensive. Each year for ten years the entire area was searched for breeding barn owls and for suitable nest sites, and the precise details of the habitat were mapped. A large number of nest sites were available, mostly in the form of disused buildings, and a population of up to 22 pairs of owls bred. Most of the grassland in the area had been improved and there were few permanent pastures or rough grazing areas. There were few ditches and the hedges were kept well trimmed. However, the area contained numerous small areas of coniferous and deciduous woodland and these proved to be the key to the barn owls' success in the area.

A sample of the birds was caught and fitted with small radio transmitters so that their movements and hunting behaviour could be studied. It was discovered that they caught about 95 per cent of their prey along the edges of the woodlands. Not all edges were suitable, however. The essential requirement was a strip of rough grassland, ideally 3 to 5 metres wide, between the trees and the field boundary fence, that could support populations of voles, wood mice and shrews.

When the habitat around each suitable nest site was examined, it was found that the owls only bred where there was at least 4 to 5 km of woodland edge within a 1 km radius of the site. Sites with less than this were sometimes occupied by single birds in winter but were never used for breeding. It was also found that the number of young produced per pair increased with the amounts of woodland edge around the nest. Using the known annual losses of breeding adults and the percentage of young that survive to replace the adults, it was possible to work out how many young must be reared per pair each year to maintain a stable population and hence calculate how much woodland edge there should be, on average, within 1 km of each nest. This worked out at about 8 to 10 km.

The species composition of the woodland seems unimportant. Similar densities of the main prey species were trapped along the edges of deciduous and coniferous woods. The crop types in the adjacent fields also seem relatively unimportant.

One problem with grassland strips around woodland is that in time they might tend to become overgrown with scrub species and hence become unsuitable for barn owls. This was not a problem in the area studied by the author, probably because high populations of roe deer prevented the establishment of scrub by their browsing. In other areas this might not happen and intervention by deliberate cutting might be needed. Research would be required to find out the most suitable way to do this, how often cutting should take place, at what time and so on.

The exact significance of other edge habitats in farmland is more difficult to assess. One striking feature of the area studied in southern Scotland was the very limited use the owls made of field edges (headlands) alongside hedges. The study area was in a typical dairy and sheep-rearing region and this meant that most of the headlands were cropped short by livestock and hence unsuitable as a habitat for small mammals. The most crucial period is in early spring when the owls are preparing to breed; at this time most headlands were bare as a result of autumn and winter grazing. The only headlands with rank grasslands in spring were those that surrounded autumn sown cereals. However, even these were avoided by the owls. The densities of short-tailed voles in these headlands were only slightly less than those along woodland edges of equal width so prey shortage was probably not the reason. Perhaps the explanation lies in the efficiency with which the owls were able to exploit headlands compared with woodland edges. Hedges offer few places to perch so the owls had to hunt in flight. By comparison, along woodland edges the owls could search and pounce from fence posts thereby saving greatly on energy expenditure. Such differences are likely to be very important when prey are scarce or when energy has to be conserved because of adverse weather conditions. Woodland edges also offer much more sheltered hunting conditions, especially during strong winds, when flight hunting is difficult. The value of hedges and their associated field headlands to barn owls is thus far from clear. In predominantly livestock areas there is little scope for encouraging the development of wide rank-grass headlands. This might be possible in cereal growing areas, but before advising farmers to leave wide headlands research is needed to understand fully how the owls would use this habitat, and also what the implications would be for the management of crop pests.

Although it is clearly possible to prescribe some changes in the farmland environment that would be beneficial for barn owls, great care is needed before implementing them. The barn owl is but one, and by no means the rarest, of the many species of farmland animals and plants that need help. If farmers are to be asked to help conserve these species (and many are eager to do so), then a balanced view must be taken so that all are catered for. For example, a woodland edge thick with brambles will undoubtedly be very beneficial to many insects, mammals and birds but not of much use to barn owls. Compromise is needed and above all farmers deserve the best possible professional advice so that they can make their contribution as effectively as possible.

The other important factor for barn owls is the availability of suitable nest sites. Provided the habitat in an area is favourable, the provision of artificial nest sites can yield successful results. For a nest box to be accepted it generally has to be erected in an undisturbed site. The ideal is a building, such as a barn or hayshed, away from the centre of activity of the farm and visited infrequently, especially in the spring. In such a location a nest box should be attached as high as possible amongst the rafters in a position that offers easy access to the birds. The design of the box is not critical but the floor space should measure at least 0.2 square metres. The entrance should be about 10 by 10 cm and, as barn owls do not gather nest material, a layer of sawdust should be provided.

In many areas there will be a shortage of suitable buildings in which to place nest boxes and the provision of nest sites will be more difficult. One possibility would be to construct an A-shaped box

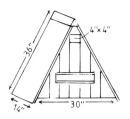

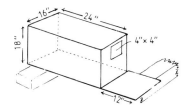

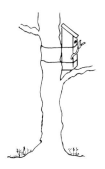
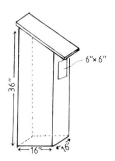

25. Nest boxes for barn owls. (Top) A dovecote-style box attached to the gable end of a farm building. Care is needed to ensure that the box is waterproof and a sliding door at the front is useful for clearing out accumulated pellet remains. This should be done every two or three years during the winter. (Middle) A standard design for use within haysheds or barns, attached as high as possible. Where the beams are narrow the box should be orientated across them such that the front platform lies over a beam — this allows the young to use the beam to exercise when they start to fly. Where wide beams are available, the box can be secured along a single beam with the same effect. (Bottom) A 'chimney' style box for use in trees where no suitable buildings are available.

similar to a small dovecote. This could be bolted to the outside of a building, preferably at the apex of the gable end and again as far from disturbance as possible. This would be quite an expensive operation. Another possibility would be to strap nest boxes to trees. This has been done successfully in southern Scotland in a joint project between the author and the Forestry Commission. Ten-gallon plastic drums were tied to spruce trees at the edges of areas of young plantation. In 1988, out of 72 such drums thirty were used by barn owls for breeding and many others were used for roosting. Tawny owls that were already in the area used some of the drums, moving from less secure sites such as old crow nests. There were no cases of barn owls being ousted but there must always be a risk that a box erected for barn owls might be used by tawny owls. There is no doubt that barn owls face many problems and it would be a very great pity if such a beautiful bird were allowed to disappear. Considerable effort will be needed to prevent such a fate.

Further reading

Cramp, S. (editor). *Handbook of the Birds of Europe, the Middle East and North Africa*, volume 4 432-49. Oxford University Press, 1985.
Mikkola, H., *Owls of Europe*. T. and A. D. Poyser, 1983.

ACKNOWLEDGEMENTS
    Photographs are acknowledged as follows: Eric and David Hosking, cover, 7, 10, 12, 13, 14, 19 (Roger Hosking), 23, 24 (Roger Hosking); Dr. C. Jeffrey, 4; J. F. Young, 6, 17, 18, 21. All the rest are by the author.